JAY LENO'S

POLICE BLOTTER

JAY LENO'S

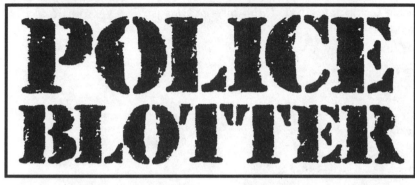

POLICE BLOTTER

Real-Life Crime Headlines from "The Tonight Show with Jay Leno"

Andrews and McMeel
A Universal Press Syndicate Company
Kansas City

Book Design by Lynn Wine

ISBN: 0-8362-1751-9

99 00 01 BAH 10 9 8 7 6 5 4

───── **Attention: Schools and Businesses** ─────

Andrews and McMeel books are available at quantity discounts with bulk purchase for educational, business, or sales promotional use. For information please write to: Special Sales Department, Andrews and McMeel, 4520 Main Street, Kansas City, Missouri 64111.

Acknowledgments

Tracy Abbott
Joe Medeiros
Dan O'Keefe
Marvin Silbermintz
Mike Colasuonno
Anne Parker
Joe Toplyn
David Lee

and *special thanks* to Chuck Martin

ANIMALS

Bunny-masked bandit sought in Pennsy heist

PERRYOPOLIS, Pa. (AP) – Wanted: middle-aged man, 6-foot-4, with full, gray beard and large, floppy bunny ears.

The description of a man who robbed a convenience store early Friday is a bit unusual, but then so was the robbery. The man wore a white bunny head with the face cut out and carried an ax.

"He wasn't going to a Halloween party," said state trooper Roy Fuller.

The bunny bandit and another man with a small revolver demanded money from clerk Jeff Dudeck at the CoGo's in Perryopolis, about 25 miles southeast of Pittsburgh, at 1:30 a.m. He handed it over.

"They fled out of the store on foot and disappeared into the night," Fuller said. "They didn't hop away."

Fuller said Dudeck had difficulty describing the bunny head. The ears, though, were clearly pink and white. And Dudeck smelled alcohol on the robbers' breath, Fuller said.

"Actually, officer, I'm just trying to get to Hef's place."

Fireman giving 'kiss of life' accidentally inhales kitty

Gannett Rochester Newspapers

"A brave fireman was rushed to the hospital for injuries suffered in the line of duty after he swallowed a tiny kitten while trying to revive it with the kiss of life," the "Sun" reports in its Sept. 7 issue. Firefighter Sven Larsen, 34, was inside a burning warehouse near Stockholm, Sweden, when he found a 6 ounce kitten gasping for air. "He ran over and started to do CPR on the kitten," Fire Chief Harald Thorensen is quoted as saying. "I was standing right next to him and the next thing I knew, he gulped real hard and swallowed the animal." The kitten did not survive, but animal rights activists plan to honor Larsen.

"That's nothing, we had a guy in here yesterday that swallowed a cat!"

INSIDE

From Wire Reports

Man found innocent of biting police dog

SAN DIEGO — A man who evaded police for 65 miles was convicted of reckless driving and other charges, but the jury said he didn't bite the police dog that stopped him.

Bronson Johns was found innocent Monday of attacking the 9-year-old German shepherd, known as Officer Faustus of the San Diego Police Department. The dog nabbed Johns after a low-speed chase on March 18.

Johns, 46, said he only opened his mouth in pain and was trying to get the dog to stop biting.

The jury convicted Johns of evading an officer with reckless driving and of driving under the influence of drugs.

"But he was wearing a mask, your honor."

A woman found a **racoon** trespassing in her garage on Garrison Road Oct. 16 at 8:30 a.m. No arrest was made.

A sick alligator was reported in a pond on Henderson Road on July 26. Police came and observed the 4-foot-long alligator. It did not look sick to them.

"How can you tell when an alligator is sick, does it wear an ice bag?"

Tuesday, May 11
9:17 a.m. - A woman in the 6600 block of Dockside reported her cocker spaniel missing. He returned about two hours later when he found out police were searching for him.

"I guess he saw his face on the back of an ALPO can."

A WOMAN ADVISED POLICE of seeing two dogs stuck together "in the act." Officer Newton was attempting to free the dogs, when "the offending dog was able to pull away, fleeing the area with a smile on its face," according to police reports. Newton reported getting the offending dog's choker chain collar, but no tags. The dog is described as black with shaggy hair, possibly a lab.

"And remember, he had a smile on his face!"

15

"Hey, he's lucky they weren't woodpeckers!"

Love birds snitch; thief is arrested

HICKSVILLE, N.Y. — A New York man was charged with petty larceny after a saleswoman at a pet shop heard birds' chirps emanating from his pants, police said.

Ruben Caro, 32, of Hicksville, was arrested after he allegedly stuffed two love birds down his pants and tried to leave the store, said Nassau County police officer Bruce Benson.

The birds, valued at $90 each, were retrieved unharmed.

16

POLICE BLOTTER

VICE

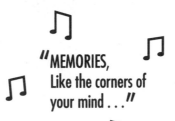

"MEMORIES,
Like the corners of
your mind . . ."

SEX CRIME

A woman was walking past a man in a parking lot when the pervert lowered his trousers and mooned her. She said she recognized the man as an old high school acquaintance.

"Going down?"

Police Log

Couple cited for sex in stuck elevator

A man and a woman were charged with disorderly conduct Saturday night after police found them having sex in an elevator.

The State College Police Department was called to Park Hill Apartments, 478 E. Beaver Ave., because an elevator was stuck between floors.

When the doors were opened, a gust of hot wind was emitted and two people, Scott O'Neill and Shelby Moran, were found partially dressed having sexual intercourse. The officer reported the couple was practicing safe sex by using a condom.

A worried mother on Northeast Verda Lane reported her 20-year-son was being chased by his girlfriend all over the neighborhood as she was ripping his clothes off. The pair ran back into the house and locked themselves in a bedroom. The mother wanted the girlfriend arrested for assault; the son wanted to be left alone. Police counseled those involved.

"From the 'I think it's called foreplay' department."

21

Couple claims crash caused conception

NAPLES, Italy – A couple of car-crossed lovers are suing an insurer for damages, claiming an unplanned pregnancy resulted from a March automobile accident in Naples' "love park."

Italian newspapers reported Friday the claim involves an accident involving a medium-sized Regata and a tiny Panda car. The accident occurred in a park that nightly attracts scores of couples who make love in their cars.

The young man claimed he and his girlfriend were engaged in sex in their small car when the large car hit it from behind. The impact made them lose control, resulting in the pregnancy, *La Stampa* and *La Repubblica* reported.

The suit demands compensation for the cost of repairing the Panda and the cost of the wedding the couple decided to have after discovering the woman was pregnant. (AP)

"Talk about getting rear ended!"

> *"So if you see a naked man wearing these clothes, call the police immediately!"*

Man exposes himself near Urbana park

by Jordan Dziura
Managing editor

A man exposed himself to a woman walking near Crystal Lake Park in Urbana on Wednesday, according to an Urbana Police report.

The victim was walking near the 100 block of Franklin Avenue at 3:23 p.m. when she noticed a man wearing no

Police roundup

clothes behind a residence. The victim said the man was standing in the yard, exposing himself to her, the report said.

The suspect is described as a white male, 5 feet 11 inches tall, 16 to 20 years old, and wearing a white T-shirt, turquoise shorts and black running shoes.

23

Redondo Beach

VIOLENT REACTION

A man walked up to a woman in the 1800 block of Hawthorne Boulevard Aug. 3 and exposed his genitals. The woman went to her car and retrieved a machete and chased the man.

POLICE BLOTTER

FIGURE THIS ONE

Suspect falters over account of robberies

By KATHRYN KRANHOLD
Courant Staff Writer

MIDDLETOWN — Robbery suspect Frank Margary can't seem to keep his mouth shut.

In some subtle, but mostly not-so-subtle statements, Margary has confessed to a spate of robberies from Bristol to New Britain to Meriden to Middlefield.

When questioned about a November robbery at Lakeside Deli & Mini Market in Middlefield, Margary told detectives: "There's no way [the clerk] could identify me, I had my hat down over my eyes."

When questioned about a November robbery in Middlefield, Frank Margary told detectives: "There's no way [the clerk] could identify me, I had my hat down over my eyes."

"Come to think of it, he couldn't identify them either!"

Ventriloquist Leaves Town — Heads of 2 Dummies Missing

Associated Press

Grass Valley,
Nevada County

Craftsman Chuck Jackson would like to know the whereabouts of two heads of dummies and an out-of-work ventriloquist who left town without saying a word.

Jackson said he suspects that the man stole the heads, which disappeared during the weekend from his home in this Sierra foothills town.

"He and $3,000 worth of dummies were gone," said Jackson, who makes his living carving ventriloquist's dummies.

The description of the heads included eyes that wink, ears that wiggle, eyebrows that go up and down and a tongue that sticks out.

One, carved of basswood and valued at $2,000, was to be shipped this week to Belgium to a teacher who planned to use it during summer school, Jackson said. The other was a $1,000 fiberglass head.

The suspected thief, whom Jackson knew only as Hector, did not take the bodies; just the heads.

Jackson said he told the Nevada County Sheriff's Department that the man said he was from Stockton.

Jackson allowed Hector to practice on several inexpensive dummies and to stay in his workshop for two days because he needed help.

"I felt like I knew him fairly well," Jackson said. "I knew him for about a year. I treated him like a brother. He ate with us at our dinner table, swam with us at the pond. We treated him well."

"Alright, now let's not jump to conclusions."

"Insufficient evidence? How embarrassing is that?"

Driver says girlfriend in lap covered nudity

JOHANNESBURG (AP) — A man charged with public indecency for driving while wearing only a shirt avoided conviction by explaining that his girlfriend was sitting on his lap.

Richard Plant, 29, was arrested after officers saw his car swerving. He admitted to a magistrate he was driving without trousers or underwear, but said his girlfriend's presence on his lap prevented his nudity from being visible to the public.

The magistrate agreed, ruling insufficient evidence to convict.

Is this a problem?

Provo Cemetery officials, in an annual press release about flower and decoration cleanup, stated, ''Anyone removing flowers from graves, other than their own, will be referred to the Provo Police Department.''

Burger Blues

Hungry Man Faces Charges

By Bill Bryan
Of the Post-Dispatch Staff

The clock read 2 a.m. as Thomas Hall headed home Monday from an evening on the town. He figured a hamburger would hit the spot.

So he pulled up to the drive-through window.

Or what he *thought* was the drive-through window.

Actually, he was placing his order for a couple of burgers and fries with a police booking clerk over the intercom at the Area III Police Station ▬▬▬▬ ▬▬▬▬.

The oddity of it all sent Officer Duane Wells outside.

There, Wells found Hall, 38, seated at the wheel of his car at the garage door entrance where officers take prisoners.

When Wells asked Hall what he doing, Hall replied: "I thought this was Burger King."

That wasn't Hall's only mistake of the night. He had alcohol on his breath and no license in his wallet.

He was arrested and charged with driving while intoxicated.

Hall, a waiter, lives in the 5400 block of Cabanne Avenue. Later in the day, he admitted sheepishly in an interview that brandy had clouded his judgment.

"I thought I was at the Burger King near my home," he said.

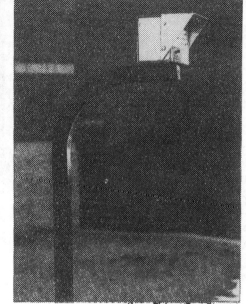

Karen Elshout/Post-Dispatch

Thomas Hall mistook this police intercom for the driveup order box of a hamburger shop.

"He should have known it wasn't Burger King when he could understand what the cop was saying."

Lawyer Billed State For Days Of Over 24 Hours

By Terry Ganey and Tim Poor
Computer Analysis by George Landau
Of the Post-Dispatch Staff
© 1992, St. Louis Post-Dispatch

There are only so many hours in a day, but not on the legal bills submitted by Forriss D. Elliott.

Elliott is one of several lawyers in St. Louis appointed by Attorney General William Webster to defend Missouri against claims by injured workers who want to be paid from the state's Second Injury Fund.

Bills submitted by Elliott show five days in the first three months of this year in which he said he worked for the state more than 24 hours each day.

The state paid all the bills, apparently without question.

March 20 was especially lucrative for Elliott, who makes $70 per hour, the standard for lawyers appointed by Webster to defend the fund.

On that day, Elliott's bills state that he spent 78.6 hours working on state cases. And that didn't include the 68.8 hours — at $35 an hour — Elliott billed for work done by his staff paralegal on that day. For the month of March, Elliott billed the state $39,051 for Second Injury Fund work.

Since June 1988, Elliott's firm has been paid more than $440,000 to defend the fund. He has received more than any lawyer except one for representing the fund. In first place is William E. Roussin Jr., who got more than $700,000 during the same period.

"From the 'anything over 24 hours a day is time and a half' department."

"Excuse me. Do you know where I can buy one of those little Christmas tree air fresheners?"

Stolen potty hits Mercedes

Dallas police are still trying to solve the mysterious hit-and-run case of the purloined potty and the smelly Mercedes.

The day before Thanksgiving someone went to a construction site in the 6500 block of Westgate Drive in Dallas and stole a porta-potty and two 100-foot extension cords. They apparently used the cords to tie the potty down on some type of truck.

A few blocks away, the cords broke and the potty fell off the back of the truck and crashed into a parked Mercedes Benz. The exact model and the amount of damage were not available Friday.

"That guy will probably never get the smell out of his car," a Dallas police officer said.

A man who was living in a trailer at the construction site told police he heard noises outside about 12:30 a.m. but didn't think anything about it.

The next morning, he realized his two cords and the porta-potty were missing.

Police gave him back the damaged extension cords and took the car and potty to the auto pound.

No one seemed to know whether the car owner's insurance covered being hit by a flying toilet.

3 suspects charged in weekend robberies

By LOUIS T. LOUNSBERRY
Courier-Post Staff

PENNSAUKEN — Three people were being held in connection with two weekend robberies, including a man whom police said wrote a robbery note on the back of his own birth certificate.

Police said the man — Ernest C. Smith, 20, of Queens, N.Y. — was charged with two counts of armed robbery and one count of conspiracy. He also was being held as a fugitive from Middlesex County, where he was wanted on drug distribution charges.

The other two suspects, Kevin D. Clark, 32, and Kevin A. Cropper, 26, both of Philadelphia, were charged with conspiracy, police said.

All three were being held Monday in the Camden County Jail awaiting a bail hearing and arraignment in state Superior Court in Camden, police said.

The trio was arrested at Eighth and Arch streets in Philadelphia Saturday night by Delaware River Port Authority police. Police had followed the car across the Ben Franklin Bridge after they received a report that it had been involved in a robbery at the Penn Queen Diner ██████████████████████ ████here, police said.

Smith is accused of walking into the diner about 5 p.m. Saturday and giving the cashier a note demanding money. He fled with the note and a undisclosed amount of money. A description of the car, which had Pennsylvania license plates, was broadcast and it was spotted by the police on the bridge.

Smith also was accused of robbing a clerk at a 7-Eleven store i███████████ ██████████████) Pennsauken at about 8 p.m. Friday. He took an undisclosed amount of cash. Again, police said, he gave the clerk a note demanding money and fled with the note and cash.

When police stopped the car in Philadelphia, they said they recovered the handwritten robbery note.

It had been penned on the back of Smith's birth certificate.

"This is the stupidest guy in the whole book!"

Drive-thru 'McThief' sentenced

By Verina E. Palmer
Staff writer

A woman who robbed the person in line behind her at a McDonald's drive-thru has been sentenced to 15 days in jail.

Rhonda A. Black, 27, of Poulsbo, also was sentenced to 250 hours of community service by a Kitsap County Superior Court judge after she pleaded guilty to first-degree theft.

The incident took place on Aug. 17 at the McDonald's restaurant in Poulsbo, when Black robbed the driver of the car that was idling behind her because she didn't have enough money to pay for the food she had ordered.

According to police, Black claimed she had a gun in her purse and robbed $20 from the person.

But police caught Black at the scene, with some help from a driver who blocked the drive-thru exit.

At the time, the city's acting police chief called it "one of the stupidest crimes in the annals of law enforcement history."

"Hey Rhonda, I'd like to fix you up with this guy who wrote his robbery note on the back of his birth certificate."

IRS tells Virginia man to cough up $68 billion

CENTREVILLE, Va. (AP) — Dave Lampson figures he'll have his new tax bill paid off in about 11 million years — not counting late fees.

His bill: $68 billion. That's billion with a "B."

"It's mind-boggling," Lampson said Tuesday. "That's more than my share of the national debt."

Lampson, a 36-year-old systems engineer, said he is paying off an old, $30,000 Internal Revenue Service debt with $500 monthly payments.

So the bill he got this week seems a tad inflated.

IRS spokesman Wilson Fadely told The Washington Post that as many as 1,000 erroneous bills with "very high figures" were mailed from the agency's Kansas City, Mo., regional office within the past week.

Fadely said the glitch occurred when someone tried to reprogram a computer to stop mailing bills to people in flood-ravaged states who have been paying off back taxes in installments.

But for Lampson, the most astonishing thing was the reaction he got from IRS officials when he tried to get the bill corrected.

"I talked to several people who didn't think it was out of line," he said. "They were very nonchalant, as if I were questioning a $100 charge."

"I'm calling about the $68 billion. Is Monday OK?"

"Your honor, I feel like I've already served my time."

Convicted Deja Vu thief faces new robbery charge

■ The suspect allegedly pulled a gun on a convenience store clerk

BY TIM O'BRIEN
Staff writer

TROY — A man awaiting a prison sentence for twice robbing a store called Deja Vu was arrested Friday and charged with the armed robbery of a convenience store.

Todd W. Bariteau Sr., 32, of Davis Drive in Poestenkill was charged with first-degree robbery and first-degree criminal use of a firearm, both felonies.

He is to be sentenced Friday in Rensselaer County Court on charges of third-degree burglary and third-degree criminal mischief.

He pleaded guilty last month to twice breaking into the Deja Vu store in Troy — smashing the same window and stealing much of the same merchandise.

He was arrested then because the same witness had spotted him both times.

According to Troy police, Bariteau — who was released on bail in the earlier incident — walked into the Xtra Mart at 493 Fifth Ave. at 3:45 a.m. Friday.

He is accused of pulling a dull silver or gray handgun and ordering store clerk Sherwood K. Politsch to open the cash register and give him all the money inside.

Politsch handed Bariteau $42 in cash, police said, and Bariteau took the money and ran west on 113th Street.

Sgt. Terrence Buchanan spotted Bariteau a short time later walking on the 112th Street Bridge. He fled from police but was arrested a short time later on the Cohoes side of the bridge.

Bariteau was arraigned Friday before City Court Judge Patrick McGrath, who set bail at $50,000. Bariteau remained in Rensselaer County Jail Friday evening, and he is due back in court at 11:30 a.m. Tuesday.

Criminal simpleton

During a holdup at a Circle K store in Waco, Texas, the robber got the clerk's attention by putting a $20 bill on the counter and asking for change. Then he pulled a gun and demanded the entire contents of the cash register. The clerk complied — giving the robber the entire contents — $15. The gunman fled, leaving the $20 bill on the counter.

Major crimes down, but some reports missing

By Kathy Farren

Major crimes in Kendall County showed a decline from 1991 to 1992, but at least part of that decline can be attributed to missing reports.

When the Illinois State Police released comparative statistics for the two years this week, Kendall County showed a 24 percent decline in major crimes (murder, criminal sexual assault, robbery, aggravated assault/battery, burglary, theft, motor vehicle theft and arson).

However, two months of those statistics from the Kendall County Sheriff's Department weren't included in 1992 figures.

Sheriff Richard Randall and the state police said the missing statistics are the result of a computer programming switch. The state's computer system wasn't able to comprehend the county's computerized information for November and December of 1992.

Without the missing two months, it appears that major crimes in unincorporated Kendall County dropped from 622 to 308.

Randall said, "We probably were down. But the true picture is the State of Illinois changed their computerized reporting system."

"Do you realize if all the reports were lost, crime could be eliminated completely!"

Police News

Three cars stolen, four are recovered

ROSELAND — Three cars were stolen and two were recovered last week in Roseland according to police.

A 1990 Pontiac was reported stolen from the parking lot of LPS Laboratories, Eagle Rock Avenue, on Thursday, June 13. The car was recovered on Saturday in Newark.

On June 12, a black 1988 Mustang was stolen from the parking lot of Automatic Data Processing (ADP).

A white 1985 Chevrolet Caprice was reported stolen from an Eisenhower Parkway parking lot on June 11. The vehicle was recovered in Newark the next day.

On June 11, a blue 1987 Chevrolet Camaro IROC was tampered with in the ADP parking lot. The driver side door lock was punched in and the steering column was damaged.

Another attempt was made to steal a car on June 13 from an Eagle Rock Avenue lot. A beige 1990 Hyundai sedan's door was broken and the ignition was punched in, police reported.

Roseland police recovered two stolen cars. Officer Steven Sargese recovered a 1991 silver Ford Escort in the parking lot of 75 Eisenhower Parkway. The vehicle was reported stolen from Newark.

Officer Kevin Kitchin recovered a stolen 1989 G.M.C. Jimmy from the parking lot at 103 Eisenhower Parkway on June 11. The truck had been stolen earlier in the day in East Orange.

"Hey, maybe they were V.W. Rabbits? Get it, three stolen, four recovered? OK. OK."

"First come, first served is right."

Brothel wins case against ballet school

MELBOURNE, Australia – A ballet school here is being forced to pack up and move following a tribunal decision that it is an embarrassment to the brothel next door. The administrative appeals tribunal heard during a protracted legal battle that the brothel, Bambra Studios, had lost clientele after the Sefra Burstin School of Dance opened next door in the middle class suburb of Caulfield. The tribunal finally ruled that Bambra studios had been there for 17 years, the two business were incompatible and it was "a matter of first come, first served".
● AFP

Calling All Cars

GOOD GUYS WEAR WHITE. A woman told Casselberry police her purse was stolen after she left it unattended on a restaurant table. Two male companions said they saw a man going through a purse in the men's room, but didn't consider it suspicious because the man was wearing a white dress.

Check thief gets 100 days in jail

By DIANE HAINES
The Herald & News

PATERSON — A Passaic County judge yesterday sentenced a 23-year-old city man to 100 days in the county jail for stealing $26,674 from a Little Falls doctor.

Superior Court Judge Sidney H. Reiss also ordered William Cusack of Lenox Avenue to serve four years probation and to make full restitution.

Cusack pleaded guilty to the charges Nov. 16 before Reiss. He admitted that while working as the office manager for Dr. Richard K. Pace, he illegally endorsed checks and wrote unauthorized checks for himself.

Assistant Prosecutor Rosemarie Gieger said Cusack admitted taking the money between Aug. 1, 1991 and March 31, 1992.

But defense lawyer Joaquin Calcines Jr. asked the court for leniency. He said Cusack's father died when he was a teenager and that his client had been helping support his mother, who also worked in the doctor's office at the time.

Calcines said the guilty plea has ruined his client's plans to attend law school and enter politics.

"Why? It hasn't stopped anybody else who's in politics!"

Police Blotter

Monday, March 9

● A man reported $12 was missing from his locker at the YMCA on Belmont Avenue. The locker was locked, but the combination to the lock was written on the back of the lock.

"Yes, but how did they get in?"

Ring reported stolen

Frank Casa of the 700 block of Parkshore Drive in Naples reported that someone stole a gold ring valued at $450, police said. The theft occurred sometime between January and Thursday.

Police Report

A bag of marijuana was found Feb. 11 on Abel's parking lot and can be claimed by the owner at the station.

POLICE BLOTTER

COPS AND ROBBERS

Police tipped to vending theft ring by suspect using quarters for bail

By JOHN SULLIVAN
Journal-Bulletin Staff Writer

PORTSMOUTH — When a man arrested early Sunday for allegedly stealing from vending machines tried to pay his bail with a knapsack full of quarters, police suspected there was more to the case.

Later, Vierra said, Rosa asked for a bright-red backpack in the pickup's cab.

When police checked the pack, they discovered about $400 in change and keys used to open vending machines. As a result, they arrested Rosa's passenger, Jason N. Perez, 20, ▓▓▓▓▓▓▓▓▓▓▓▓▓▓ Both were charged with larceny, receiving stolen goods and possession of burglar's tools.

"Is that a roll of quarters in your pants or are you just happy to make bail?"

NOT CUT OUT FOR CRIME

Burglar can't hurt anyone

Police say that Jim Babcock of Pittsburgh tried to break into a shed, but cut his hand punching out a window. So he decided to do a garage instead, climbed a tree, went in an upstairs window — and fell through a hole to the first floor. There, he stumbled into a grease pit and "split his head wide open," police said. Why do we get the feeling Mr. B was a little, uh, disoriented?

Then he broke into a house, falling down the cellar stairs, scraping his arm and leg. Possibly sensing it wasn't his night, he jumped in his car to leave — and hit a tree, banging his head on the windshield.

He got out of the car, carefully locking the door, went back to the garage, and — we swear this isn't a joke — fell into the grease pit again. He went back to his car, but couldn't find the keys, so he broke a window, climbed in — and broke his gearshift. Getting the car started somehow, he raced down the block — into another tree.

Police found him unconscious in the car, his face pushing the horn button. He was convicted of breaking and entering.

"I think I can, I think I can ..."

"From the 'good alibi' department."

Police log

BROCKTON — When police told 20-year-old Alex Pauleus of 25 Hunt St. that a woman had identified him as one of three men who burst into an apartment on Court Street late Saturday night and held the occupants at gunpoint, he said that was impossible.

"How could she tell it was me? I had a mask on," he reportdly told police.

The victim, who was in the second-floor apartment at 216 Court St. when the three armed men forced their way in, said Pauleus was carrying a handgun.

Police release sketch of armed robber

SHOREHAM — State police have released a composite sketch of an armed bandit who robbed the Shoreham Service Center on ████████A at about 3 a.m. Jan. 24 and fled on foot with an undisclosed amount of cash.

The bandit, who wore a mask, carried a revolver, troopers said. A small vehicle with a mismatched front fender and a broken taillight might have been involved.

The suspect is a white man, with blond hair and dark eyes. He is about 5 feet 10 inches to 6 feet tall, 180 pounds, Sgt. J. Ron Winn said. The suspect spoke in a deep voice and wore his hair in a "bowl cut," Winn said. The bandanna on his face was red, black and white, Winn said.

"Oh that guy! Of course!"

Easton police describe suspect in armed holdup

Easton police have released a composite drawing of a suspect in an armed robbery last week at the Wawa market in the city's College Hill section.

Police described the suspect as either Hispanic or a light-skinned black male, about 25-30 years old, with brown eyes and a thin mustache. The bandit weighed about 170-180 pounds and was wearing a navy blue ski mask, blue windbreaker and jeans. Police said he entered the store around 2:10 a.m. Jan. 8 armed with a small caliber black small frame automatic pistol.

He demanded money and left on foot with an undetermined amount of cash. No vehicle was seen.

Anyone with information on the robbery is asked to call city detectives at 250-6635.

Composite of robbery suspect

"Stop the presses, SPIDERMAN has turned to life of crime!"

•On Nov. 18 a man wearing a sweatshirt with the hood pulled tightly over his head and a mask covering all but his eyes pounded on the front door of the Security Federal Savings Bank in Durham, N.C., scaring employees inside. After several loud attempts to push open the door, which is a ''pull'' door, he fled. Durham police say precisely the same thing happened at another bank on Oct. 22.

"This is the kind of guy that would get stuck on a broken escalator."

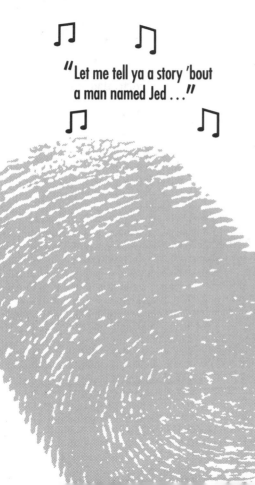

"Let me tell ya a story 'bout a man named Jed ..."

Keystone Krook: And now, the dumbest bank robber of the month.

According to Point of View, a magazine published by the Alameda County District Attorney's office, the guy walked into an Oakland bank and handed the teller a note reading, "This is a stikkup. Hand over all yer mony fast."

Guessing from this that the guy was no rocket scientist, the teller replied, "I'll hand over the cash as long as you sign for it. It's a bank policy: All robbers have to sign for their money."

The guy thought this over, then said, "Uh, I guess that's OK." And he signed his full name and address.

And that's where the cops found him a few hours later.

Two arrested for recent housebreaks

80 breaks since Sept. from Vt. border south

HILLTOWNS— Two brothers, now living in Springfield but with ties to the Route 66/County Rd. area of Huntington, have been arrested in connection with a series of daytime house breaks in the Hilltowns.

Raymond Arel Jr., 21, and his brother, Steven, 19, both of 27 Phoenix St., Springfield, were arrested by the State Police yesterday and arraigned on a number of charges including breaking and entering in the daytime, larceny over $250, and larceny from a building.

Raymond Arel was arrested by officers working out of the Springfield Barracks while Steven Arel, accompanied by a 13-year-old juvenile listed as a missing person by the state Dept.

(continued on page 17)

"Ebony and Ivory..."

DRUG DEALER ROBBED: A city man told officers he was attacked Tuesday night and robbed of the $200 he had made selling drugs that evening, police said. Carlos Rodriguez, 22, of the 1200 block ████████████████, was jumped by three teen-agers in the 300 block of N. Franklin St. about 10:45 p.m., police said. The trio punched Rodriguez, hit him with sticks and stole his cash, police said. He declined medical treatment.

"Is this covered under your homeowners policy?"

Randall Yeager, 32, of Milpitas, Calif., was arrested in July after passersby chased him as he allegedly fled from a bank he had just robbed in Fremont. Yeager, 5 feet - 6 and more than 300 pounds, had tired after running a few dozen yards from the bank and had slowed to a walk by the time the pursuers caught up to him.

"Good plan, take the money and walk."

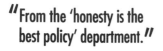

"From the 'honesty is the best policy' department."

■ Raymond Moyher, 30, was arrested in West Haven, Conn., in November after a police officer stopped him near a WaWa convenience store that had just been robbed. According to the arresting officer, when he asked Moyher what he had been doing, Moyher said, "I just left the WaWa store that I robbed."

NEWS OF THE WEIRD

BY CHUCK SHEPHERD

DONNA Clark, 26, and Paul Kramer, 31, faced charges in Merchantville, N.J., in April when Clark allegedly grabbed $216 worth of film and walked out of a drugstore. The couple's names were provided by their 6-year-old son, who was in the store at the time but who was forgotten by the couple as they made their getaway.

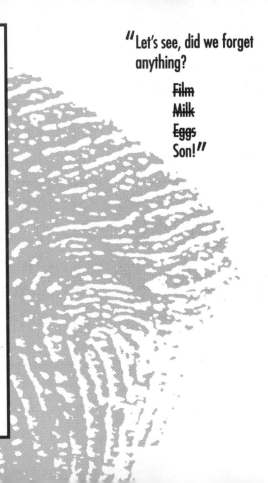

"Let's see, did we forget anything?

~~Film~~
~~Milk~~
~~Eggs~~
Son!"

Burglar to have plenty of time to watch 'Boys

BY MONICA STAVISH
Fort Worth Star-Telegram

GRAPEVINE — Overcome with Cowboys fever, a bold burglar pilfered a color television from somebody's home to watch Sunday's game against San Francisco, police say.

Then he went back for the remote control.

Now the 24-year-old man is being held by Grapevine police in connection with about 50 burglaries. And he will probably have to watch the next Cowboys game, the Super Bowl, in jail.

Police declined to identify the man or two women they believe to be accomplices.

"He's a big fan of the Cowboys and he didn't have a TV, so he set about finding a TV so he could watch the Dallas-San Francisco game," Detective Ben Flanagan said. However, after getting the set home, the suspect told police, he <u>realized that the remote control would make the game more enjoyable.</u> So he returned to the house and took that, too.

■ **The rush is on:** Scalpers circle Texas Stadium . . . . . . PAGE 21A

"Gee, do you think he went back again for the batteries?"

Anti-theft unit tagged for thefts

NEW YORK (NYT) — Six years after New York City created a unit to stop thefts from parking meters, 20 members of that unit have been charged with stealing $1 million in quarters in the last two years.

City investigators said yesterday that one-third of the staff of the agency that collects money from the city's meters each had plundered up to $1,500 a day in coins, which they usually hauled off in canvas bags they secretly carried. One collector boasted to an undercover city investigator that he had stolen $45,000 in two years, officials said.

"Within those five hours," said Ellen Schwartz, a city inspector general, "they were able to steal the money, place the quarters in paper rolls, drop off the money at their homes or convert the quarters into currency at banks, and still find time to go to the office and play cards."

The transportation department formed the 61-member parking meter service unit in 1987 after 35 employees of a private company that collected the money were arrested on charges of stealing almost $1 million.

The city's 67,000 parking meters provide about $47 million in revenue each year, transportation department officials said.

"Is that a roll of quarters in your pocket or are you just happy to see me?"

"Next time use a plastic bag and tie it firmly around your neck."

Robber Almost Bags Himself

JACKSONVILLE — An inept robber who wore a paper bag over his head in a holdup attempt this week may still be using the disguise — out of embarrassment.

The bag had holes cut in it to allow the robber to see. But it shifted during the crime, leaving the man in the dark, Charlie's Supermarket clerk Keetek Dore said this week.

Then, when the man moved the bag back into place, it ripped and exposed his face — showing that he was a regular customer of the store, Dore said.

"I yelled, 'Bob!' " Dore said. "Then he ran away."

The would-be robber also needs to learn how to give orders.

Before his disguise ripped, Dore said, the man had demanded, "Give me the register!" Dore said she didn't know whether he meant that he wanted the whole register or just the money in it.

"I said, 'What?' and he said, 'Give me the register!' I said, 'What?' again. Then the bag broke open," she said.

Would-be robber calls 911 for help

Man needed way out of locked bank after breaking in

DURHAM, N.C. (AP) — A man who got stuck inside a building and couldn't get out did what most people would do — he dialed 911.

But police say this man was a would-be bank robber who was thwarted both in attempts to steal money and get out of the bank.

"He called 911 and said he got in and couldn't get out. He wanted the police to come and get him out," Durham Police Sgt. M.C. Supples said Tuesday.

The man was waiting inside First Union National Bank when officers arrived. The man called 911 at 2:52 a.m. Tuesday.

"I've never had an experience like that," Supples said. "When I got there, I saw a 3-foot by 3-foot hole in a window by the night deposit. There was glass all over the parking lot."

Dispatchers kept the man on the phone until officers arrived and then told him to go to the window with his hands up.

"He was real cooperative," Supples said.

The man apparently used a large rock to break the thick window glass. He crawled in the window and landed on a desk inside the bank.

"He said he broke in and went through the teller drawers and couldn't find any money. He said he was afraid he would be cut if he tried to go (back) out through the window," Supples said.

Supples and Officers R.M. Davis and D.P. Ailstock used a metal flashlight to break the remaining glass out of the window. The officers were then able to rescue the man through the window.

"I think he just wanted some help and didn't know how to get it or couldn't get it," Supples said.

Authorities said Larry Shelton James of Durham was charged with breaking and entering and was being held in jail under a $25,-000 bond.

Escapee's phone call likely led to capture

ASSOCIATED PRESS

STINNETT, Texas — A Georgia prison escapee captured after 17 years on the run says he probably led authorities to his home when he called the FBI trying to find out whether his escape was still under investigation.

After escaping from Georgia's Jefferson County Correctional Institute in 1975, James Sanders started a new life in Texas, got married and had a daughter.

He was arrested by federal agents Jan. 24 at his home in the northern Texas community of Fritch, about a month after he called the FBI. Sanders, without identifying himself, had asked questions about a man he described as a friend who escaped from prison in 1975.

Sanders, 42, said his 11-year-old daughter and wife of almost 16 years were unaware of his past, which includes a 1974 conviction on three counts of burglary and two counts of theft. He maintains his innocence of the charges.

"From the 'didn't this guy ever play hide and seek' department."

65

Robbery Suspect Caught After Using Marked Bills

Federal officials Thursday were able to identify a Philadelphia native as the suspect in the Sept. 3 robbery of the downtown Scranton branch of the First National Community Bank of Dunmore after he paid his rent with marked bills taken in the robbery.

Assistant U.S. Attorney Barbara Kosik Whitaker noted that federal authorities were able to identify Darryl Williams as the suspect in the Sept. 3 robbery after his landlady deposited the bills in the Oak Street branch of Pioneer American Bank.

Whitaker made the comments following Williams' initial appearance Thursday on armed robbery charges before U.S. Magistrate-Judge Thomas Blewitt.

Without objection from Williams' attorney, federal public defender Patrick Casey, Blewitt ordered the defendant held pending a preliminary examination set for Oct. 6.

Blewitt noted, however, that the examination may not be necessary should a federal grand jury choose to indict Williams in the meantime.

Williams was brought to Scranton after federal authorities tracked him down in Philadelphia.

Whitaker said authorities traced Williams to Philadelphia after his landlady deposited marked bills in a local bank and identified the suspect as the person who had given them to her. Williams was residing at ▬ Wood St. at the time, the prosecutor said.

Because Williams had moved to Scranton from Philadelphia, authorities concentrated their search there and were able to apprehend him after talking with some of his friends there.

According to Whitaker, Williams was on parole for an armed robbery in Philadelphia at the time he robbed the First National Community Bank here.

Williams reportedly entered the bank with a knife and told a teller to give him money or "I will shoot your head off."

If convicted of the charges, Whitaker said, Williams could be sentenced to a maximum of 25 years in prison and fines totaling $250,000.

"Or maybe I'll stab you with my gun!"

66

"Hey, didn't I just see you at the bank!"

Tired-looking robber brandishes a knife, threatens to shoot

A man armed with a knife threatened to shoot a clerk at a James Street motel Thursday morning before escaping with about $140 in cash, police said.

No one was injured during the 6:15 a.m. heist at the Days Inn at 1100 James St.

A Days Inn desk clerk told police a man who looked like he had not slept in several days, asked about the cost of a room. Then the man pulled out a butcher knife, climbed over the counter, and threatened to shoot the clerk, according to police records.

Least competent person

Suspected purse-snatcher Dereese Delon Waddell in suburban Minneapolis last winter stood on a police lineup so the 76-year-old female victim could have a look at him. When police told him to put his baseball cap on his head with the bill facing out, so as to be presentable, he protested, "No, (I'm going to) put it on backwards. That's the way I had it on when I took the purse."

Robbery Suspect Mugged

A man stole $2,100 from a Brooklyn savings bank on Friday but was mugged as he made his getaway, so he immediately reported the crime to the nearest police station house, the police said. Officers promptly arrested the man.

"He said that he had a robbed a bank and that he himself had been robbed," said a police spokesman, Sgt. Norris Hollomon. "Only a psychiatrist would know why he did it," he added.

Friday at 3 P.M., the man, identified as Anthony Colella, 49 years old, of ██████████t in the Bensonhurst section of Brooklyn, entered the Independence Savings Bank at ████████ in Bath Beach. He handed the teller a note saying, "Be fast. I have a gun. . . Give me all your money. Don't make me pull it," the police said. Taking $2,100 and stuffing it into a brown paper bag, he then escaped on foot but went only as far as 16th Avenue and 86th Street.

As he was walking along, an unidentified man jumped out of a station wagon, shoved Mr. Colella and grabbed the paper bag containing the $2,100 before driving off, he told the police. Mr. Colella went to the 62d Precinct station house at 1925 Bath Avenue to report both crimes.

The station wagon mugger has not been found. The police have charged Mr. Colella with first-degree robbery, criminal possession of stolen property and criminal possession of a weapon.

"Hey, that's my stolen money, come back here!"

"Police estimate damage at approximately 99 cents."

Man found inside store on Public Square

Wilkes-Barre Police arrested Steven Wayne Zaremba, 29, Saturday night after he was found inside The 99¢ Store, 15 Public Square.

Police responded to the store's burglar alarm and found Zaremba inside the building. A 2-by-8 foot window was shattered at the store front.

Zarmeba, address unknown, was charged with burglary, criminal trespassing and criminal mischief and was arraigned before the on-duty magistrate.

He was lodged in Luzerne County Correctional Facility overnight.

Suspicious circumstances: An Aries Place N.W. resident called police Tuesday evening, after she found a muddy handprint on her sliding glass door. When the officer learned the woman had been gardening, he compared her hand with the print and found they were the same.

"That's not all, her prints are all over this place!"

Shoplifting *mich.*

SAULT STE. MARIE — Ryan
Joseph Labine, 20, of ███████
████ was arrested at mid-
night Thursday for shoplifting a
package of condoms and an early pregnancy kit from a supermarket on the I-75 business
spur, city police report.

At the same store, at 2 a.m.,
Bryce Kelly Parker, 18, ████
███████ LSSU, was arested
for shoplifting a can of potato
sticks valued at 36 cents while
purchasing other items, police
reports said.

POLICE BLOTTER

FROM THE TRAFFIC BEAT

Two chase after stolen truck, sit on suspect awaiting police

By Kate Thompson
Journal staff writer

A cellular phone can be handy if you want to call police while you're sitting on a suspect.

Sioux City police were unable to respond quickly to a report of a truck stolen from Foulk Brothers Plumbing and Heating, ▓▓▓▓▓▓▓▓▓▓▓▓▓▓ Owner Bill Foulk said the other owner and an employee waited about 20 minutes and then went looking for the truck themselves.

It didn't take them long to find it.

"They were on West Fourth Street and they looked over toward West Third Street and there went the truck up the street," Foulk said.

The two chased in their vehicle and the stolen truck pulled over. Three men were inside.

"The driver and a passenger got away, but the gentleman in the middle tripped and they sat on him until the police came," he said.

Capt. Peter Groetken said the original call about the stolen truck came in at 3:52 p.m. but no officers were available to take the call. Dispatchers put out a general broadcast about the stolen pickup truck within three minutes and dispatched an officer at 4:11 p.m.

A few minutes later, Foulk's partner called police by cellular telephone to tell them they had recovered the truck and captured a suspect in the parking lot of the HyVee Store on Cook Street.

Carlos Arciaga, 26, a transient, was arrested on a charge of second-degree theft, a felony.

Foulk said his partner should have called police while they were following the truck instead of stopping it and attempting to catch the thieves themselves.

"They could have had a gun or a knife," he said.

Police are investigating the theft and looking for the other suspects, Capt. Pete Groetken said.

"Sounds like a case of Jake and the Fatman."

A Creston man was run over by a cow while he was riding his bicycle at the corner of Sycamore and DeVoe streets at 3:22 p.m. Saturday.

According to a police report, Donny Johnston, 612 E. Grand Avenue, was uninjured after a cow ran over him while he was riding his bike. The bike was a total loss.

The cow had escaped from the Creston Veterinary Clinic, 509 W. Townline Road.

"How did the cow escape? Did he tunnel under the building?"

● Two teenagers riding bikes hit a police car at Heritage and Josey Thursday when they tried to stop short. One of the teens went under the car with his bike and the other managed to swerve. One of the boys told police he had no brakes on the bike because it made it more interesting that way.

"Kind of like living life with no brains."

"I wonder if his left blinker was on?"

Robber nabbed after slow driving

ANGOLA, Ind. — A 71-year-old man charged with robbing a bank at knife point was being held Thursday on $500,000 bond.

Police said Ted Shively of Angola was arrested Wednesday after police noticed he was driving too slow.

He was stopped about 5 minutes after Star Financial Bank was held up. Police said he was driving away from the scene about 20 miles an hour.

A set of hubcaps were stolen from a Mazda in the 9200 block of US 377. The car was not moving when the hubcaps were stolen.

"These criminals just keep getting smarter and smarter, don't they?"

"The Club," an anti-car theft device, was stolen from a vehicle in the ▮▮▮▮▮▮▮▮ of Tustin East Drive. A coat hanger was possibly used to gain entry.

"Gee, do you think they used a radio to get into the car to get the club?"

"Gee, maybe the passenger door was unlocked?"

A CONROE MAN reported to police between 10 p.m. on Saturday and noon on Sunday, someone stole his Jeep.

The 1985 CJ7 Jeep valued at $2,500 and bearing Texas license plate number ██████████ was reported stolen from the Bent Tree Apartments Phase II at ███ North Interstate 45, McCreary said.

Police do not know how entry into the car was made, but said the driver's side door had been removed from the vehicle by the owner prior to the theft.

❷ IN APPLE VALLEY, assault with a deadly weapon was reported at 5:53 p.m. Tuesday on Otoe Road near Sago Road. A woman said that about 30 minutes previously she had been driving an ice cream truck when another ice cream truck tried to run her off the road. She said the other truck was her competition. No damage was reported.

The name game comes up a loser

Fort Worth Star-Telegram

The Dallas driver's idea was to give the police a phony name so they wouldn't connect him with an outstanding traffic warrant. The trouble is he gave the police the name of a guy wanted in Fort Worth for murder.

The 29-year-old man was stopped by Dallas police yesterday on a traffic violation. It was then that he came up with the name of a man wanted in connection with a 1991 stabbing death.

After being brought to Fort Worth and told he was under arrest for murder, the man confessed to making up the name, police said.

He was released after officers verified his identity. No charges were filed when the man promised to settle his outstanding warrant, police said.

"My name? Why it's Charles Manson. Yeah, that's it, Manson."

83

Driver just a hunka, hunka burning rubber

By The Associated Press

DICKSON, Tenn. — An Elvis Presley look-alike from Canada was arrested after two state troopers' cars were rammed during a high-speed chase.

Andre Guay, 34, of Quebec was charged with attempted murder, reckless driving, vandalism, leaving the scene of an accident and evading arrest, said Tennessee Highway Patrol spokeswoman Karla Ricn.

Rich said Guay, who speaks French and little English, has black, "Elvis-style" hair and was wearing a jacket that reads "Elvis Lives" on the back.

WKRN-TV in Nashville reported that Guay told officers he became distraught over marital problems and "became even more distraught after visiting Graceland," the late Presley's Memphis home.

Rich said Trooper Allen Brenneis saw a car crossing the median of Interstate 40 near Dickson, 34 miles west of Nashville. He pulled the car over, but the driver backed his car into the cruiser, and the high-speed chase began.

After 17 miles, the speeding Oldsmobile rammed into a patrol car at an exit ramp, Rich said. Trooper Jim Hutcherson suffered a broken leg and toes and was to undergo skin graft surgery today.

POLICE BLOTTER

THE HOLIDAYS

Woman denied time to spend with parents

The Associated Press

MINNEAPOLIS — A woman free on bail after admitting that she tried to hire a hit man to kill her parents will not be allowed to spend Christmas with them, a federal judge has ruled.

U.S. District Judge Diana Murphy said she sympathized with Heidi Steiro's desire to be with her parents, but turned down the request Friday even though her parents wanted to see her.

Earlier this month, Steiro, of St. Anthony, admitted that she instigated the murder-for-hire scheme but pleaded guilty to a lesser charge of making a threatening phone call. She is free on bail while awaiting sentencing but is prohibited from seeing her parents, though she talks to them frequently by phone.

Assistant U.S. Attorney Joan Lancaster said she has concerns about the safety of Steiro's parents.

"Apparently, Mom and Dad want her back," Lancaster said. "To be so forgiving of somebody who has hired somebody to kill you I find quite remarkable."

Steiro, 21, was arrested in September after she offered an undercover officer $45,000 to kill her parents and made a phone call to make sure they would be home on the weekend she wanted them slain, authorities said.

Steiro, who was working as a lab technician at the University of Minnesota, told authorities she stood to inherit $2 million.

Crime Watch tree stolen

A decorated Christmas tree was stolen Tuesday from a tree stand in the New Marshfield Park across from the post office, according to the Athens County Sheriff's Department.

The tree belonged to the New Marshfield Crime Watch.

> OFFENSIVE SNOWMAN, 700 block of Menomonie St., officers corrected problem. Reported at 4:45 Saturday.

"This sounds like a job for Lorena Bobbit!"

■ Child's snowman is stolen

PENSACOLA — Micki Clifford said her 6-year-old granddaughter was heartbroken when three men in a truck pulled into the yard Saturday and stole the snowman she had built with her grandfather.

She said the truck was filled with about a dozen snowmen.

— A Tribune Wire Service Report

"They're probably taking 'em to Mexico, they get big money for 'em down there!"

"Hey, I just saw 12 of 'em in a truck, headed for Mexico!"

POLICE LOG

Items found

■ Assorted scarves, hats and gloves, as well as a small wheelbarrow and several straw brooms were found Sunday morning in an alley off Sunnyside Avenue. The items appear to have been taken from snowmen. Anyone with the above items missing should call Wyomissing police.

STRANGE NEWS BRIEFS

Man arrested eating tree bark

FRANKFORT, Ind. (AP) — A 20-year-old man was arrested and charged with chewing the bark off the trees on the courthouse square.

"The statement he gave me was that he was showing off for the kids who were out there," Detective Chuck Toney said.

Brian K. Lyman was charged with two counts of criminal mischief, each punishable by six months in jail and a $1,000 fine.

Lyman was arrested Sunday after the mayor demanded an investigation into why several recently planted trees were damaged. Toney said he went to the square, where teen-agers pointed out Lyman as the guy he was looking for.

He was accused of causing up to $6,000 in damage.

"I told him he would have been better off going to Red Lobster," Toney said. "At least it wouldn't have cost him as much."

Lyman also admitted biting the ends off light bulbs on municipal Christmas trees, the detective said.

•Cozette Wright, 35, was charged in May with stabbing her daughter, 20, on Mother's Day in Omaha, Neb., after an argument over who was the better mother. •

"Is there a Hallmark card for this?"

News of record

City Police

•Police are investigating the theft of a 50-pound pumpkin reported taken Sunday from Winn-Dixie supermarket. Police reports describe the pumpkin as orange in color, with a face drawn on it.

"No, I'm sure we ain't never seen anything like that around here. Orange, huh?"

94

POLICE BLOTTER

FOOD AND DRINK

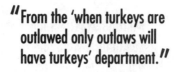

"From the 'when turkeys are outlawed only outlaws will have turkeys' department."

Disturbance – Domestic

1200 blk. Sacramento Ave. Male subject is throwing turkey at female. Respondent says she is a dead woman if police don't arrest him this time.

Police nab banana bandit

Associated Press

ANCHORAGE, Alaska
A man armed with a banana in a bag couldn't give police Sgt. Mark O'Brien the slip.

The robber held up seven convenience stores, groceries and fast-food restaurants early Thursday with a concealed banana.

O'Brien arrested Randy Baldwin, 31, of Anchorage after a brief chase. Baldwin was arrested on seven counts of armed robbery.

"We can't wait until the weekend, my banana will be rotten by then!"

Bank robber bluffs teller with bananas

BURBANK — A robber used a bunch of bananas yesterday to hold up a bank, and made off with an undisclosed amount of money, police said.

A police bomb squad discovered the ruse after evacuating 22 people from the Security Pacific Bank.

The well-dressed bandit, who held up the bank about 9:45 a.m., left behind a bag, which he told a teller contained a bomb. Police found that the bag contained three bananas — and a bite had been taken out of one of them.

United Press International

"From the 'don't say you weren't warned' department."

OR

"Stand back or you're all going to slip and fall."

Don't drink the coffee

Employees of the Merita Bread Co. in Greensboro, N.C., noticed last year that their company coffee machine produced a foul-tasting brew, and they tried various remedies to improve the taste. Some employees then remembered a heated dispute they had had with a delivery man, who had access to the plant in evening hours, and thus organized a stakeout. Dale David Tinstman, 46, was later arrested for having urinated into the coffee machine daily for several months.

— Universal Press Syndicate

"And don't eat the yellow snow."

OR

"And this non-dairy creamer tastes kind of funny, too!"

Two charged for Ex-Lax cupcakes

Associated Press

WILLMAR, Minn. — Two women who allegedly gave a co-worker cupcakes laced with laxatives got a result they didn't expect: The cooks now face felony charges.

Gail Lynn Dalaska and Heather Marie Kramer, both of New London, are accused of baking two tainted cupcakes for another woman for her birthday. She ate one and was violently ill for two days.

The two women pleaded innocent Friday in Kandiyohi County District Court to charges of adulterating food. Their employer, the Jennie-O Foods turkey plant in Willmar, also suspended them for two days after the incident.

According to a criminal complaint, the women baked six Ex-Lax pills into each of the two cupcakes Sept. 19. The victim was later told by one of the defendants that they had put the laxatives in the cakes as a practical joke.

The court ordered a Dec. 27 trial. The defendants remain free on their own recognizance.

Mocha cures space fears

FAIRFAX — A woman asked to talk to a Marin sheriff's deputy about space aliens with large hats who were trying to get in her body again.

A deputy visited her after getting the call at 10:10 p.m. Saturday. After talking to her, the woman said she would feel better if she went out and got a coffee mocha, said Lt. Russ Hunt.

In July in Ogden, Utah, a Japanese college exchange student, angry that a Baskin-Robbins store had just shut its doors for the evening and would not serve him, suffered a laceration on his buttocks when he pressed too hard on the window while mooning the store's employees.

"Make that 32 flavors."

● "WE WERE disgusted," Ted Varey, a Belper pensioner, told reporters. "My wife's no prude, but finding two coconuts and a massive cucumber

arranged in an obscene manner on our car bonnet brought on her shingles. This is the last straw. Last week there was a root vegetable rammed up the exhaust pipe also in a suggestive manner. We had to call the AA out."

The incident was the last in a series of obscene fruit displays that have been mysteriously appearing on local cars, the work of a prowler known to the police only as 'General Gherkin'. "Usually it's just an apple, an orange and a banana," explained a spokesman from Mackworth College, "but now the General's started getting nasty. That last cucumber was over a foot long."

A spokesman admitted that police were baffled, but promised that all greengrocers in the Belper area would be interviewed. *(The Belper Express, 8/7/93. Spotter — Hugh Binns)*

"Hey, this peach has got fuzz on it. Call the police!"

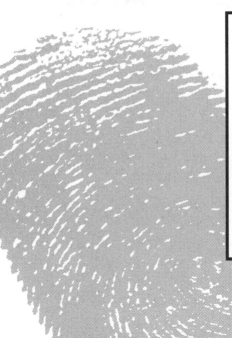

"Cigarettes and a pepperoni, I guess he must be having friends over."

Suspect: Woman saw something else

A man used a pepperoni for an excuse when he was accused of exposing himself to a woman Thursday.

The woman, a 28-year-old Monroe resident, reported to Monroe police that the man followed her around while she was inside an area party store about 10 p.m. Thursday.

When she went to her car, the suspect was sitting in his vehicle. He allegedly exposed himself to her. Police said the victim got into her car and drove off. Reports said she wrote down the man's plate number and called police.

Police contacted the suspect, a 43-year-old Luna Pier man. He said he was inside the store and bought some cigarettes and a pepperoni. He told police he did not expose himself and the woman must have seen the pepperoni.

Indecent exposure charges might be sought.

Candy-wrapper trail led cops right to him

ELYRIA — Police say the lure of chocolate was too much for a 22-year-old Elyria man to resist.

Darrell Bugg of 328 S. Maple St., was charged with breaking and entering and accused of stealing a box of candy from a laundramat at 1502 West Avenue.

Police found most of the candy by following a trail of Butterfinger, Kit-Kat and M&M wrappers from the store, a police report said.

The incident began at 11:30 p.m. Saturday, when police were called to the business and found a door leading to the store standing open.

There was no one inside. A man nearby told officers he saw a man wearing a gray outfit and carrying a box in his arms run out of the store, heading south on West Avenue, police said.

Police found Bugg a short time later, near West Avenue and Oberlin Road. He was wearing gray pants, a gray shirt and black winter gloves, something police said they thought unusual for the weather conditions, a report said.

Bugg was held at the Lorain County jail, waiting to be arraigned in Elyria Municipal Court today.

"From the 'never go shopping when you're hungry' department."

Thief takes off with Lucky Charms cereal

BARTLETT — A Bartlett woman in the 500 block of Deere Park reported recently that her box of Lucky Charms cereal was stolen, according to Aug. 27 police reports.

"Come to think of it, the pot of gold is missing too!"

Police solve case of the missing bacon

A Grand Rapids resident told police last week that someone had entered his home during the night and taken five pounds of bacon from the refrigerator.

Upon further investigation, police discovered his wife had gotten up for a late night snack, but was afraid to admit it.

"Can you blame her? If you ate five pounds of bacon would you tell anyone?"

VANDALISM: The manager of a convenience store called deputies after two men were spotted setting fire to a donut in the parking lot. When the manager approached them, he reported they threw crumbs and dirt at him.

"Burn? I can't even keep my donut lit!"

❖ Agence France Presse reported in June that a middle-aged woman in Lausanne, Switzerland, fainted in a supermarket, and medical assistance was summoned. A nurse decided to unhook the woman's bra so she could breathe better, discovered a shoplifted frozen chicken in the bra, and concluded the woman had fainted from the cold.

Crime Watch

Strange donuts

The Troy Police Department said they received a call from a local donut shop regarding some odd phone calls on Nov. 8.

An employee of the Dunkin' Donut store located at 4977 Livernois said a customer repeatedly called the store asking "strange questions about strawberry donuts."

Police are describing the caller as a 35-year-old man, 5-feet-10 inches tall and weighing 200 pounds with black curly hair.

"How did the cops know what he looks like? Is there a standard profile for strawberry donut abusers?"

Man accused of Spam theft

By MARK ENGLAND
Tribune-Herald staff writer

POLICE REPORT

Waco police filed robbery charges against a man accused of trying to sneak out of a grocery store with 20 cans of Spam.

Harold Montgomery, 30, was in the McLennan County Jail Tuesday night under a $20,000 bond set by Justice of the Peace Alan Mayfield.

A checker spotted a man walking out of the H-E-B Store at 1102 Speight Ave. with a lump under his coat. When the checker tapped the man's coat, he heard cans rattling together, according to the police report.

The man tried to run, but the checker grabbed the coat. Spam rained on the sidewalk. During the struggle, the man reportedly struck the checker on the left shoulder.

The checker was not injured.

Sgt. Dennis Kidwell said the struggle resulted in the shoplifting charges being upgraded to robbery.

"If a suspected shoplifter just pulls away and runs, there probably wouldn't be enough to charge him with robbery," Kidwell said. "But if he makes a threatening gesture or strikes someone trying to stop him, it changes the charge to robbery."

"It's a crime wave!"

It's no baloney: Police seek lunch meat vandal

For the second time in as many days, a home on Longview Drive in Lisle has been the recipient of unsolicited luncheon meat.

Lisle Police Department reports stated that a can of Spam was left on the doorstep of a home on the 2600 block of Longview Drive between midnight and 8 a.m. Tuesday, April 13. The Spam was found sitting on a piece of paper with the word "SPAM" written on it.

On April 12, a resident of the same block of Longview Drive reported finding a pile of sliced ham at 9 a.m. by the front door of his home. The sliced ham was sitting on a piece of looseleaf paper with the word "HAM" written on it.

"But how can you replace the sentimental value?"

Wednesday, June 9

A toaster and two Pop-Tarts were damaged during a toaster fire at 8:49 a.m. in an apartment building on the ▓▓▓▓▓▓▓▓▓▓▓▓ Police assisted the Lisle-Woodridge Fire District in responding to the call. Damage to the toaster was estimated at $25. The Pop-Tarts were valued at 50 cents.

GATES

- A Burning Brush Drive resident reported that sometime between 2:30 and 8:30 p.m. July 15 someone broke into his home by smashing a window.

The resident also discovered that a box of Pop Tarts had been opened and that one was missing. The victim said the suspect also might have used the pool table.

Nothing else appeared to be missing.

"What do Spam and Pop Tarts have in common? Crooks love 'em!"

Potato vandalism reported

The Club at Pelican Bay, 707 Gulf Park Drive, North Naples, reported that someone carved an obscenity into an Idaho potato in the club's kitchen, sheriff's deputies said.

Other minor vandalism was reported. The incidents happened Sunday or Monday, reports said.

"When will this senseless violence end?"

Fire calls

- Hot dog fire on a stove ███████ ████ at 8:08 p.m. Tuesday. The owner forgot putting the hot dogs on the stove and left the residence. Damage to the hot dogs estimated at $2.

"Good thing he had the one dollar deductible."

"Why did the chicken cross the road? I guess we'll never know."

2:21 p.m. — Suspicious circumstance, Red Top Road. Report of meat that had been thrown all over road was a chicken that had been run over.

POLICE BLOTTER

THE BIG HOUSE

Accused thief wears victim's stolen suit to court

By James L. Smith
Citizen Patriot News Service

FLINT — A man who wanted to impress the judge hearing his felony case wore a custom-made suit to court.

Unfortunately for Michael S. Allén, the olive-green, double-breasted suit wasn't his.

In fact, police say, the suit actually belonged to the man who had come to Flint District Court to testify against Allen.

Allen, 26, and another suspect were facing felony charges of credit card fraud, carrying a concealed weapon and auto theft after their Oct. 3 arrest.

The gun carried by Allen's alleged accomplice had been stolen from a Groveland Township house a few weeks earlier; the victim of that burglary was called to court to testify about the theft of the weapon, said Mundy Township Det. Tom Hosie.

The suit Allen wore to court was among the items taken in the burglary, Hosie said.

Hosie added Allen wore a sweat suit underneath the suit to fill it out because it was a few sizes too large.

Without knowing who Allen was, the burglary victim walked up to Mundy Township Police Chief David Guigear and Hosie and asked if Allen was involved in the burglary case. When the officers asked why he wanted to know, the man replied: "Because he's wearing my suit."

"Uh, your honor, could I have a word with my client first?"

121

Tampa, Fla., school officials invited inmate Edward McIntyre, serving 90 years for kidnapping and assault, to a local high school to make an inspirational speech to students for Law Day in February. (While there, he escaped through a restroom window.)

"Who better to speak on law day than a criminal?"

Inmates must get own keys, regulations say

WELLINGTON, New Zealand (Reuter) — Every prisoner's dream could come true in New Zealand — new building safety regulations say jailbirds will have to be given the keys to their cells.

The tricky question came to light when police applied for a building permit for a new station in rural New Zealand, Police Regional Commander Murray Jackson said Wednesday. Under a building code introduced this year, people in custody must have immediate access to exits in case of a fire.

"It means that if you have to put prisoners behind lock and key, you have to give them a key so they can get out," said Jackson.

"Ok. Here's your key, but it's only for emergencies, like in case you need a few bucks or something."

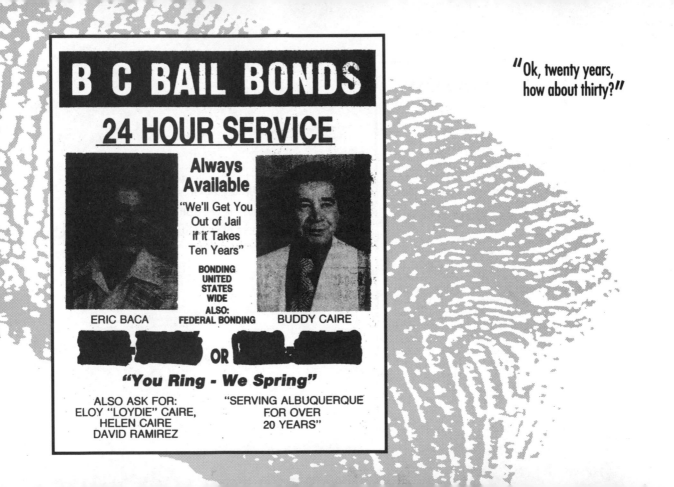

"Ok, twenty years, how about thirty?"

Man Gets Life In Prison For Running Drug Ring From Prison

"Talk about job security!"

LIFE STORY

In Orlando, Fla., Judge Ted Coleman declared: "I am sentencing this man to prison for the rest of his life, with credit for the 34 days already served. (Well, OK!)

"From the 'thanks for nothing' department."

Gilbert Franlin Rhodes - First Degree Murder, sentenced to serve the rest of his natural life in the Department of Corrections of New Mexico, followed by 2 years parole

"From the 'I think it's time to get a new lawyer' department."

OR

"So when I die I'm free to go?"

From the *Morning Star* archives

March 14, 1893: "It is not lawful now for the prisoners in Massachusetts State prisons to carry concealed deadly weapons. If they are caught carrying them they will be arrested and put in jail."

POLICE BLOTTER

HAVE GUN WILL TRAVEL

Toy gun scares robber using toy gun

By Dawn Bracely
Democrat and Chronicle

Rochester police on Friday arrested a toy-gun-toting robber who was scared off by the toy gun of one of his victims and then hit on the head by a bat-wielding neighbor.

Michael West, who also goes by Michael Smith, 29, of 93 Bartlett St., was charged with first-degree robbery, second-degree assault and fourth-degree grand larceny and third-degree criminal use of a firearm, police said.

Eddie Nassar, 76, and his 72-year-old wife, Freida, got out of their car on Gardiner Avenue at about 8 p.m., when police said West approached them, and stuck what looked like a gun to Nassar's neck and demanded money.

Lt. Al Joseph of Genesee Section said the robber reached into Nassar's pocket and grabbed his keys.

Nassar's wife pulled out her own toy gun and pointed it at the robber and said, "Leave my husband alone. You'd better drop that gun or I'm gonna shoot you," Joseph said.

West pleaded with Freida Nassar not to shoot him, threw the keys to the ground and started to run away, pushing the elderly couple to the ground, Joseph said.

Joseph said as the robber ran south on Gardiner Avenue, a neighbor who heard the commotion threw a baseball bat at the man, knocking him to the ground.

The robber got back up and continued running, with blood dripping from the wound on his head. Five police officers followed the trail of blood behind buildings, over fences, through parking lots and along Chili Avenue, Joseph said.

The robber had stopped at the home of an acquaintance who gave him paper towels to stop the bleeding, but didn't let him inside her house. Joseph said when the robber spotted police, he took off for another house. A woman at this second house called police.

'It's just a lot of people helping out that let us catch this guy," Joseph said. "When we got to the house, where he was bleeding when the girl helped him, we were able to get his name."

West was arrested and taken to St. Mary's Hospital.

"Where did this robbery take place, Toontown?"

Man shot in head blows the bullet out his nose

By KAREN FERNAU
Phoenix Gazette

CHANDLER, Ariz. — A man who had been shot in the head during a traffic dispute blew the bullet out of his nose in a hospital emergency room.

The victim, a 25-year-old Chandler man, was riding in a car when he was shot above the right temple by an angry driver at 1:25 a.m. Sunday.

While at Desert Samaritan Medical Center in Mesa, the victim's nose began bleeding, and he expelled a .22-caliber bullet.

"One of our officers who went with him to the emergency room handed him a towel, and (he) blew the bullet out," said Sgt. Steve Spraggins, a police spokesman.

"It was a freak kind of accident in which the bullet did not hit the brain, but apparently lodged in his sinus cavity."

The man's fiancee, who was driving when the victim was hit, asked that the couple's names not be printed because the man suspected of shooting her boyfriend has been released from jail.

"Hey, this Nyquil stuff really works!"

132

"It's not the size, it's what you do with it."

Man robbed of small gun by pair with bigger gun

Larry D. Piortt, 30, ██████████████ ██████, reported he was robbed by two men at gunpoint of $63 and a .22-caliber pistol while walking at Plum and Columbia streets about 12:10 a.m. Wednesday, police said.

Piortt said the men approached him and one pointed a .38-caliber revolver at him and demanded money. When he gave the man the money the other one frisked him and took his pistol, it was reported.

Gary Blantz, 29, was arrested for kidnapping a bar owner near Lancaster, Pa., in February. Police reported later that Blantz shot himself in the foot with his .45-caliber revolver to show the victim what would happen to him if he were disobedient.

Man shoots himself in foot 3 times cleaning guns

PRINCETON, W.Va. (AP) — A man accidentally shot himself in the right foot while cleaning each of three handguns, police said.

The 38-year-old man was drinking beer Wednesday morning when he decided to clean his guns, according to a report filed by Mercer County Sheriff's Deputy L.R. Catron.

His .32 caliber handgun went off, but it "didn't hurt" so he finished cleaning the .32, then began cleaning his .380 caliber pistol, which also went off, said the report, which didn't name the man. That bullet "stung a little, but not too bad," Catron quoted the man as saying.

The man finished cleaning the .380 and then pulled out his .357 caliber pistol, only to shoot himself a third time. The man finally called an ambulance. Catron said the man told him the .357 shot "really hurt because the bullet was a hollow point."

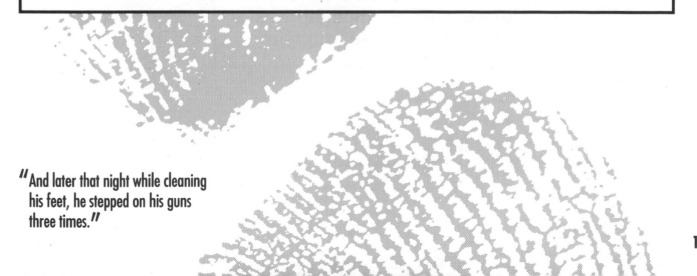

"And later that night while cleaning his feet, he stepped on his guns three times."

An off-duty police officer at a tavern accidentally shot another officer in the neck when he fired a miniature gun he thought was a lighter. Police released no names.

"No names? How about Beavis and Butthead?"

"You'd probably only get half of that for it."

OR

"DUH ... I knew that."

POLICE BLOTTER

■ Danny Simpson, 24, was convicted of a March bank robbery, which brought him $6,000, in Prince Albert, Canada. Police later informed him that the gun he had used was a collector's item worth as much as $100,000.

•Ronald Melvin Gower, 31, was arrested in Princeton, Ky. in July, after he tried to rob the First Bank and Trust Co. with a toy gun. One teller refused to hand over money, and as the robber tried to persuade her, another employee, who happened to be carrying a Polaroid camera to take a picture of a car later in the day, snapped the robber's picture. At that point, Gower allegedly backed away, said he was just kidding, and asked for change of a $100. (Gower was wearing a rolled-up stocking under his baseball cap, to use as a mask, but had forgotten to pull it down over his face when he entered the bank.)

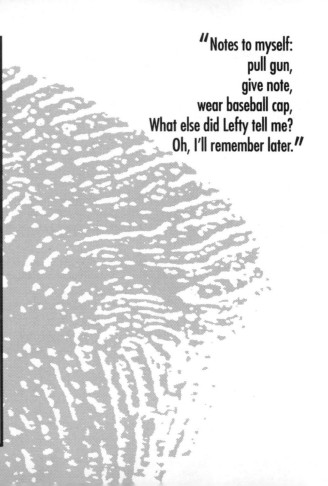

"Notes to myself:
pull gun,
give note,
wear baseball cap,
What else did Lefty tell me?
Oh, I'll remember later."

POLICE BLOTTER

JUST PLAIN NUTS

$50 million bill given for cab fare, police say

No cab driver would have change for $50 million.

But that's how one fare allegedly tried to pay for his $35.95 cab ride, Indiana State Police said Thursday.

Rodney Amos, 22, of Indianapolis was arrested on charges of forgery and theft after allegedly attempting to pay his fare with a fake $50 million bill that had a picture of President Bush.

About 9 a.m., Metro Cab driver Albert Lee called police to U.S. 40 near Six Points Road in Hendricks County, said Trooper Irwin Falk. Amos allegedly offered the bill in payment for a ride from the Eastside of Indianapolis to Plainfield.

Amos told Lee he intended to pay his bill but needed change. Lee offered to provide the change, and Amos handed him the phony money, police said.

The bill appeared to be an altered $1 bill, they said. Amos was released from the Hendricks County Jail in the custody of a relative.

"Everybody knows a $50 million bill has Dan Quayle on it."

■ FRANKLIN COUNTY

Man wielding spatula robs store

A spatula-wielding robber held up a Franklin County convenience store early yesterday, state police at Chambersburg said.

Police said the unidentified man fled with an undisclosed sum of money.

The clerk at the Scotland Fuel convenience store on Black Gap Road in Greene Twp. told police the man entered the store at about 3:23 a.m. Saturday, wearing pantyhose over his face and possibly lipstick.

When the man approached the counter, he displayed a spatula with a dark handle and demanded money, troopers said.

The robber was described as white, in his early 20s, about 5 feet 2 inches to 5 feet 6 inches tall and weighing about 140 pounds. He has a thin build and unknown hair color, police said.

Police believe he may have fled toward State Route 696 in a gray, early- to mid-1980s mid-sized station wagon.

A blue and white flannel shirt he was described as wearing was found on a northbound exit ramp onto Interstate 81, police said. He also wore blue jeans and a dark T-shirt under the flannel shirt.

"Be careful, his wheelman could be hiding a skillet!"

"When you absolutely, positively, have to be there tomorrow!"

Area in brief

Police return woman to sender

New Philadelphia police officers played mailman early this morning when they assisted a mail delivery — they helped a woman out of a mailbox at 2nd St. and E. High Ave.

According to reports, the woman's foot became stuck in the box shortly after midnight when she tried to "mail herself to Mississippi, Ala."

The woman said she wanted to see her boyfriend there.

"Hey, I could have had a V-8."

Thief steals urine sample

LISLE — A thief entered an unlocked Airborne Express van parked in either the 900 or 1000 block of Warrenville Road and stole a urine specimen from a lab envelope left inside. No one has been arrested in the incident, police said.

"Kiss me, quick!"

Would-be gas thief gets a real mouthful

A man who tried to siphon gas from a motor home got a mouthful of sewage instead, Seattle police said.

Police got an early morning call last week from the owners of the vehicle parked on a Seattle street, police spokeswoman Vinette Tishi said.

When officers arrived, they found sewage and what looked like vomit on the ground. Nearby they found a man curled up ill next to a car.

Tishi said the man admitted he was trying to snitch some gas and plugged his hose into the motor home's sewage tank by mistake.

The motor home owner, from Bellingham, declined to press charges, calling it the best laugh he's ever had, Tishi said.

Suspect loses breath after chase

A La Grange man who allegedly shoplifted 27 packs of cigarettes in Downers Grove Tuesday was arrested after he ran out of breath during a chase with a security agent.

Devoe L. Harris, 27, was taken to Good Samaritan Hospital in Downers Grove after he told police he was having difficulty breathing.

Harris reportedly was seen stuffing the cigarettes down the front of his coat near one of the cash registers at Cub Foods, ███████████ in Downers Grove. When he was confronted by a security agent outside the store, he allegedly pushed the agent and took a swing at him before he ran into a nearby residential neighborhood.

Police said the security agent caught Harris when he ran out of breath. Harris was charged with retail theft, battery and obstructing justice.

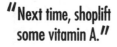

"Next time, shoplift some vitamin A."

Ridge

- A woman called police when she found an upside down turtle on her front lawn at 11 a.m. June 1. The officer told her to turn the turtle right side up. She did but called back to report that the turtle had no arms, legs or a head. The officer told her not to worry, and the turtle fled in an unknown direction before police arrived.

"I don't know which way he went, officer, it all happened so fast!"

Stranger than fiction. In June, a lawyer won a $3,000 settlement against the J.C. Penney store in Newport, Ore., over an underwear purchase. The man claimed that after he wore the shorts for the first time, a tag, "Inspected by No. 12," stuck to his penis so firmly he could not remove it.

After soapy water and rubbing alcohol failed, he went to a doctor, who removed the sticker with an adhesive dissolver. That caused a rash, however, and when it disappeared, it left a scar in the shape of the sticker.

The settlement compensated him for lost work time and for marital strife.

Universal Press Syndicate

"And when he gets excited, it becomes 1,285,365,994!"

Men charged with stealing 18 Preparation H boxes

Three men were arrested Wednesday, July 28, in connection with the theft of several boxes of Preparation H suppositories from Jewel/Osco, ████████████

According to St. Charles Police, an employee saw one of the men remove an entire display of Preparation H suppositories and stuff them in his shirt and pants. He and another suspect ran out of the store and jumped into a car that was waiting outside.

The three men later were arrested by Batavia and Geneva police officers in Batavia. Police found 18 boxes of Preparation H in the car, along with 25 boxes of pain reliever.

The following were arrested for felony retail theft: Michael Rosas, 18, of Hoffman Estates, Amos Harris Jr., 37, of Maywood and Marvin Lee Harris, 34, of Hoffman Estates. Police said their bail was set at $7,500 each.

"Will the defendant please rise?
I'm already standing, your honor!"

Absolutely quackers

A Tulsa, Okla., physician, writing in a 1992 issue of the Irish Journal of Psychological Medicine, reported on a 32-year-old woman whose neighbors had just had a large satellite dish installed in their yard. The woman became convinced that she was being wooed by Donald Duck and that the dish had been placed there to facilitate his communicating with her. She spent lots of time "hovering" around the dish and eventually undressed and climbed into it, where she later said she consummated marriage to Mr. Duck.

"It's a trick! That's not a satellite dish, it's a giant wok, get out of there!"

COMPELLING EXPLANATIONS

⇨ IN MAY, THE MISSOURI COURT OF APPEALS turned down David Turner's appeal of the automatic suspension of his driver's license for refusing to take a blood alcohol test. His argument to the court was that, when arrested, he was too drunk to realize that he should have submitted to the test.

"Yeah, no fair. Maybe I could have passed!"

"Jeff! Don't take the riding mower, you'll kill yourself!!!"

Man guilty in mower DUI case

HAGERSTOWN (AP) — A man who was driving a lawn mower towing a wagon containing beer pleaded guilty to his sixth drunk driving offense.

Jeffrey Scott Haines, of Hagerstown, pleaded guilty yesterday in Washington County District Court to driving under the influence, refusing to sign a citation and destruction of property.

Haines, 29, was spotted driving the lawn mower without its lights early July 3, said Sheriff's Deputy Tracey Payton.

Deputy Payton said Haines ignored him at first and then refused to get off the mower when stopped.

"At that point, Haines ordered his dog, Ben, to attack the deputy," said Assistant State's Attorney Andrew Kramer.

Instead, the dog walked over and soiled the deputy's trousers. Damage was estimated at $188.

Accused chewed on shorts

STETTLER (CP) — David Zurfluh tried to eat his undershorts on the theory the cotton fabric might absorb the alcohol in his stomach before he underwent an RCMP breath analysis.

He found out Thursday it was a wasted effort.

The 18-year-old from ██████ appeared in provincial court and was acquitted on a charge of impaired driving because the breath analysis showed his blood alcohol level exactly at the legal limit of .08 milligrams per 100 millilitres.

Zurfluh was collared by RCMP Const. Bill Robinson after he ran from his vehicle, which had been seen weaving down the highway, and was put into a patrol car.

Zurfluh told Judge David F. MacNaughton he ripped the crotch out of his shorts as he sat in the car, stuffed the fabric in his mouth and then spat it out.

Students from a local high school, in court to view the workings of the law, had difficulty maintaining their composure when the testimony grew lively, and were removed by their teacher.

"People were leaving the courtroom with tears in their eyes," said RCMP Const. Peter McFarlane.

"He thought his breath was bad before!"

153

A Bird Lane resident reported on July 25 that suspicious people had anchored a boat behind his house and were walking on his beach. Police found the boat was not anchored but was moving and the people were not walking on the shore. They were water skiing offshore.

"Hey, Mister, glasses in about an hour, try it!"

Theft ... An exotic dancer at Le Place on the 700 block of West Avenue in Jenkintown told police that three black G-strings valued at $100 were stolen from the ladies room while she performed. A suspect described as a white female, 40 years old, heavy-set with a burn on the side of her face, fled on foot, police said.

"So that's Victoria's secret."

Bizarre callers give 911 operators a jolt

■ Male is sexually stuck to a dog and cannot get loose.

■ Meet complainant regarding a neighbor's rabbit eating complainant's garden.

■ Complainant says unknown male has been living in her house. Complainant is partially blind and just found his clothing.

■ Complainant says her rose bushes have been trimmed and thinks the neighbor did it. (Sgt. Katz's aside: "I wish I could find the suspect on this one. He can come trim my roses anytime he wants.")

■ Complainant says several males came onto property and rode her sheep.

■ Complainant says the Rev. Jesse Jackson is refusing to leave her house. (Mr. Jackson was not in Dallas at the time, Sgt. Katz noted.)

■ Meet complainant regarding a gested the man turn his TV off.)

■ Female caller wants police to come and get her. Asked why she needed police, she says: "Because it's raining, and I rode my bike to the store. I need them to take me home, or my hair will get wet."

■ Male caller says a light in the breezeway of his apartment building had been broken out. Wants police change it.

■ A caller reports a male dressed like Elvis Presley is kicking another man while yelling, "You ain't nuthin' but a hound dog."

■ Intruder broke into an elderly woman's home. Asked to describe the man, the woman said: "Well, he resembles Elvis Presley — but when he was slender, not fat."

Staff writer Jennifer Nagorka covers law enforcement for The Dallas Morning News.

"So it's true, Elvis is alive and kicking!"

Man faces charge of drunken driving

Police charged a Waltham man with driving under the influence of alcohol after they found his 1979 Ford pickup lying on its left side on Harvard Street in Newton early Saturday.

The man allegedly told police that the truck tipped, after he drove over "a large hump." But police said investigators quickly determined that the "hump" was a Hyundai coupe parked on the side of the road.

The driver, Gordon H. Loftus, 32, of ▓▓▓▓▓▓▓▓▓▓▓▓ was arrested at 12:40 a.m., police said.

"From the 'Have you driven a Ford . . . lately' department."

Forged lottery ticket would have won $5,000

ASTORIA, Ore. — A forger failed to check an Oregon Lottery Monopoly ticket altered to win only $1, missing out on a legitimate $5,000 win.

The error was discovered when a woman presented the forged ticket to a convenience store clerk last week, claiming it was $1 winner.

"The clerk looked at it and said it's not a $1 winner, it's a $5,000 winner," said Officer Denise Kotaniemi of the Astoria police. "She was floored. She said, 'This is great.'"

But a second look revealed that a number had been altered to make the ticket appear to be a $1 winner, voiding the legitimate $5,000 combination, Kotaniemi said.

The woman left the store without identifying herself.

"Your mom was right: If you cheat, you're only hurting yourself."

Early Monday morning, April 6, a Hayfork woman requests to talk with a deputy because her housekeeper is not putting her towels away properly.

"Boy, that Leona Helmsly just doesn't quit!"

*"Never mind the medication,
I know what I saw!"*

9:50 p.m. Petty theft: A woman advised that she felt her purse had been taken from a bathroom at a business on the 100 block of Sir Franciso Drake Boulevard by an unknown subject who had beamed it out of the room. She also stated she hadn't taken her medication today.